..... Kids-Life .....

DEVOTIONS

Kids-Life DEVOTIONS

STORIES THAT APPLY BIBLICAL TRUTH TO REAL LIFE

Chariot VICTOR
PUBLISHING
A DIVISION OF COOK COMMUNICATIONS

Chariot Books is an imprint of ChariotVictor Publishing
A division of Cook Communications, Colorado Springs, Colorado 80918
Cook Communications, Paris, Ontario
Kingsway Communications, Eastbourne, England

KIDS-LIFE DEVOTIONS

Unless otherwise noted, all Scripture is taken from the *Holy Bible, New Life Version,* Copyright © 1969,
1976, 1983, 1986, Christian Literature International, P.O. Box 777, Canby, OR 97013. Used by permission.

Scripture quotations marked (TLB) are taken from *The Living Bible*, © 1971, Tyndale House Publishers,
Wheaton, IL 60187. Used by permission.

Scripture quotations marked (ICB) are taken from the *International Children's Bible,* New Century
Version, copyright © 1986 by Sweet Publishing, Fort Worth, TX 76137. Used by permission.

Scripture quotations marked (NIV) are from the *Holy Bible, New International Version.* Copyright © 1973,
1978, 1984, International Bible Society. Used by permission of Zondervan Bible Publishers.

Previously published as *Kids-Life Sleepytime, Anytime with God.*

Cover illustration by Rick Incrocci

First hardcover printing, 1994
First paperback printing, 1998
Printed in Singapore
02 01 00 99 98   5 4 3 2 1

• • • • • • • • • • • • • • • • • •

These commandments that I give you today

are to be upon your hearts. Impress them on your

children. Talk about them when you sit at home

and when you walk along the road,

when you lie down and when you get up.

Deuteronomy 6: 6,7 (NIV)

• • • • • • • • • • • • • • • • • •

CONTENTS

• •

• • • • • • • • • • • • • •

"Train a child in the way he should go ..."

Proverbs 22:6 (NIV)

Dear Parents,

Teaching your children to become strong young men and women of God is the most important legacy you can give them. Children will learn from you readily as you read to them, but sometimes it's hard to find just the right story to read that will both entertain and teach them.

The *Kids-Life Devotions* book will help you do both. It includes a wide variety of fun stories to read with your children, arranged by Bible-based, character-building themes so you can find just the right story for the right occasion. This book also invites young readers to "read it myself" with large, easy-to-read type and a second-grade reading level.

Easy-to-use parenting helps follow each story. They include:

•**Kids-Life Questions**—to help you talk with your children about the character-building theme from the Bible and help apply it to their lives.

•**A Bible verse** that presents the same theme as the story. Read the passage aloud or memorize it together as a reminder of the lesson.

•**A prayer** to help your children start talking to God about what they are thinking and feeling.

Enjoy this book as you read and learn together with your children.

The Editors

Kids-Life™

God and Me

Hey, Kids!

The following stories are all about God and you. They'll tell you about His wonderful creation, His love, and how He can be your best friend.

Think about It

You are special to God. He loves you. He wants you to love Him too. Maybe you could sing a song, draw a picture, write a poem, or pray a special prayer to let Him know just how much you love Him.

Remember This

This is how God showed his love among us: He sent his one and only Son into the world that we might live through him. I John 4:9 (NIV)

To the Grown-Ups

The foundation for life is knowing and accepting God's love. Take every opportunity to remind your child of this unconditional love. Encourage your child to express his love for God in childlike ways—and your faith will be increased as you experience God's love through the eyes of a child.

God Made Everything—Just Right!

A Story about Creation

God made the sky.
He made it . . . JUST RIGHT!
> He made the moon, the clouds, the stars,
> the sun, the planets.

God made the sky.
He made it . . . JUST RIGHT!

God made the land.
He made it . . . JUST RIGHT!
He made the grass, the rocks, the hills,
the mountains, the deserts.
God made the land.
He made it . . . JUST RIGHT!

God made the water.
He made it . . . JUST RIGHT!
        He made the oceans, the rivers,
        the lakes, the brooks, the rain.
God made the water.
He made it . . . JUST RIGHT!

God made the fish.
He made them . . . JUST RIGHT!
        He made the salmon, the tuna,
        the cod, the trout, the shark.
God made the fish.
He made them . . . JUST RIGHT!

God made the animals.
He made them . . . JUST RIGHT!
    He made the cow, the horse,
    the dog, the cat, the lamb.
God made the animals.
He made them . . . JUST RIGHT!

God made the birds.

He made them . . . JUST RIGHT!

    He made the sparrow, the robin,

    the sea gull, the dove, the eagle.

God made the birds.

He made them . . . JUST RIGHT!

God made the trees.

He made them . . . JUST RIGHT!

    He made the fir tree, the fig tree,

    the pine tree, the palm tree, the oak tree.

God made the trees.

He made them . . . JUST RIGHT!

God made you.

He made you . . . JUST RIGHT!

 God made your eyes, your nose, your
 mouth, your arms, your legs.

God made you.

He made you . . . JUST RIGHT!

God made everything!

 He made the sky, the land, the water, the
 fish, the animals, the birds, the trees.

And God made you.

God made everything . . . JUST RIGHT!

Kids-Life™ Questions

- What can you see in the sky that God made?
- What is your favorite animal? Why?
- Why do you think God made so many different kinds of animals, birds, and trees?

From the Bible

In the beginning God made from nothing the heavens and the earth.

. . . And God made man in His own likeness. In the likeness of God He made him. He made both male and female.   Genesis 1:1, 27

Prayer

Dear God,

Thank You for making me . . . JUST RIGHT!

In Jesus' name, Amen.

God Gives Us Colors

A Story about Creation

The world we live in
Is not black and white.
God filled it with colors,
Some pale and some bright.

The grapes on the vine,
Dark purple and sweet,
Are not hard to pick
And great fun to eat.

The orange-colored fruit
Is perfectly round,
Like the orange sunset
That seems to touch ground.

Greens, yellows, and
blues—
On the butterfly's wing—
God's provided a wealth
Of colors that sing!

For sweetest perfume,
God gave us red roses.
And when we smell them
They tickle our noses.

Ribbons of sunbeams
Give off yellow glows.
They help keep us warm
Right down to our toes.

His animals, birds,
Grand flowers, and more,
Are God's gift to us
Of colors galore.

Kids-Life™ Questions

• What is your favorite color?
• What did God make in that color?
• What can you think of that is more than one color?

From the Bible

The earth is the Lord's,
and all that is in it,
the world, and all who
live in it.
Psalm 24:1

Prayer

Dear God,
Thank You for my favorite color, _____.
In Jesus' name, Amen.

My Favorite Kind of Love

A Story about God's Love

How many kinds of love are there?

Sometimes my new gray kitten falls asleep on my pillow. She feels soft and warm against my cheek. She purrs when I scratch her ears. "I love you, Kitty," I say. Taking good care of my soft gray kitten is one kind of love.

My brother Danny eats raspberry ice cream. He eats a lot of raspberry ice cream. Sometimes Danny says, "I love raspberry ice cream!"

Eating raspberry ice cream is another kind of love, I guess.

Yesterday Dad brought home fourteen yellow daisies with a pink bow. (I know there were fourteen because I counted them.) He gave the yellow daisies with the pink bow to Mom. He gave her a kiss too.

Yellow daisies with a pink bow and kissing is another kind of love.

One time, last Tuesday I think, in the middle of the night, my nose got stuffy. I started to cough. I started to cry.

Mom came into my room. She gave me a drink of water and a hug. She rocked me in Daddy's big brown rocking chair and I fell asleep.

My mom loves me.
That's one of my favorite kinds of love.

Mom and Dad always tell Danny and me about God's love. God is the One who made yellow daisies and raspberry ice cream and the whole world! He even made you and me.

Then God sent His only Son, Jesus, to tell us how much He loves us.

He loves us more than I love my soft gray kitten. He loves us more than my dad loves my mom. He even loves us more than Danny loves raspberry ice cream!

Jesus came into the world to say, "God loves you very much!" And because Jesus came, there will always be God's special kind of love in the world.

There are many kinds of love. But God's love is the best kind of love.

Kids-Life™ Questions

- How many kinds of love do you think there are?
- What's your favorite kind of love?
- How do you know that God loves you?

From the Bible

For God loved the world so much that he gave his only Son so that anyone who believes in him shall not perish but have eternal life.   John 3:16 (TLB)

God loves us so much He gave us His Son. That's the best kind of love.

Prayer

Dear God,
Please help me to always remember how much You love me. In Jesus' name, Amen.

The Good Shepherd

A Story about Faith

"I want to be a good shepherd, Grandfather," said Sari.

"Shepherding is an important job," said Grandfather. "When King David was a boy, he looked after his father's sheep. When he was a man, he looked after God's people."

"A good shepherd finds green grass and water for his sheep," said Grandfather. They led the sheep through the morning to the hidden places in the hills where the green grass grew.

Sometimes the trails were steep. Once, a little lamb slid down onto a ledge and bleated loudly for its mother.

Sari lay on her belly and reached down with her grandfather's crook. She caught the lamb by the front legs and pulled it to safety.

At noon they rested by a deep pool of clear water. Sari had brought bread, cheese, and dates for lunch. Grandfather had a leather jug of goat's milk.

"A good shepherd watches over his flock," said Grandfather. The sheep were sleeping in the sun.

Sari saw something moving in the hills. "Grandfather! What's that?"

"It's a hungry wolf," said Grandfather. "You have sharp eyes, Sari."

Sari fitted a smooth stone into her sling. She spun the sling, and the stone flew through the air. It landed just behind the wolf. The wolf ran away into the hills.

"A good shepherd leads his sheep to safe resting places," said Grandfather.

They walked down the steep trails. When they reached a little stone corral, Sari counted each sheep to make sure none were missing. Grandfather checked to make sure none were hurt.

Sari was tired. Being a good shepherd was hard work.

"Grandfather?" Sari said. "There is no door in the pen. The sheep could get out, or the wolf could get in."

Grandfather smiled. "I am the door, Sari," he said. He lay down across the opening with his blanket. "The sheep will not step on me, and I will not let any wolves in."

Sari snuggled into her blanket. "We are taking good care of the sheep, Grandfather." Far off in the hills the hungry wolf howled. Sari shivered. "But who is taking care of us?"

"Do you remember the words of King David, Sari? 'The Lord is my Shepherd . . .' He is watching over us, little lamb. Go to sleep."

Sari, the shepherdess, fell asleep under the stars.

Kids-Life™ Questions

• What are some ways Sari and Grandfather took care of the sheep?
• Who takes care of you?
• How does God take care of you?

From the Bible

The Lord is my Shepherd. I will have everything I need. Psalm 23:1

God will always take care of us. He is our Good Shepherd.

Prayer

Dear God,
Thank You for always watching over me and always taking care of me. In Jesus' name, Amen.

God Whispers to Me

A Story about God's Love

I love to laugh and shout and play, and sometimes Mother says to me, "My, but you are loud today."

But I love to listen too.

I love to listen to the whisper of the leaves in the trees, to whispers in the grass from tiny winds that pass.

I love the whispered ripple of the brook on its way to the sea. It seems to have a special song just for me.

I love the sleepy whisper of the birds as they say, "Good night, I'll see you with the morning light."

I love to go out in the dark to listen to the whispers of nighttime things, of owls and crickets and locust wings.

And sometimes when I'm very still I think I hear God whisper in my ear, "You are My child. I love you. I am near."

Kids-Life™ Questions

- What do you like to listen to in the daytime?
- What do you like to listen to at night?
- When do you listen to God?

From the Bible

Yet day by day the Lord also pours his steadfast love upon me.   Psalm 42:8 (TLB)

Prayer

Dear God,
Please help me to listen to the quiet things in Your world. In Jesus' name, Amen.

Jesus—My Very Best Friend

A Story about Friendship

If I went down in a submarine
till the starfish blinked
and the sun turned green,
way down deep in the deepest sea
I know who would be there with me—
Jesus, my very best friend!

If I decided to climb Pikes Peak
to hike for a day
or even a week
and the woods were dark and full of bears—
I'd talk to Jesus. I know He cares,
'cause He's my very best friend!

If I rode a rocket to the stars
to play on Pluto
or march on Mars
or chase a comet all over the place—
Jesus would be there.
He made outer space
and He is my very best friend!

When I'm a pirate in a pirate suit,
with a pirate ship
and rich pirate loot,
and my sister asks if she can play,
I think to myself, what would Jesus say?
'Cause He's my very best friend!

I once threw a tantrum, a terrible fit,
and Mommy paddled me
right where I sit.
I was afraid I'd made Jesus sad—
I told Him, "I'm sorry," that I had been bad,
AND . . .
He was STILL my very best friend!

JESUS MY VERY BEST FRIEND

If I could . . .
I'd go to Portugal, Paris, or Spain
to meet all the children
so I could explain,
"There's someone who will be with you
wherever you are
whatever you do—
Jesus, YOUR very best friend!"

Kids-Life™ Questions

- Where is your favorite place to talk to Jesus?
- What do you think Jesus would say if you asked Him if you could play?
- Who loves you and forgives you no matter what you do?

From the Bible

The angel said to the women, "Do not be afraid. I know you are looking for Jesus Who was

nailed to the cross. He is not here! He has risen from the dead as He said He would. Come and see the place where the Lord lay."
Matthew 28:5,6

Jesus is alive and
He is your best friend
wherever you go!

Prayer

Dear God,
Today, please help me to tell _____ that You are our very best friend. In Jesus' name, Amen.

Kids-Life™
My Family and Friends

Hey, Kids!

The following stories are all about kids like you and their families and friends. They'll show you how God wants you to treat other people.

Think about It

Sometimes even when you *know* what's right, it's hard to *do* what's right. Take helpfulness, for example. Maybe Mom asks you to help by putting your games away or setting the table. It's easy to grumble and pretend you didn't hear her, but that's not the way God wants you to act. Sometimes it helps to ask yourself how you want other people to treat you. If you want other people to help you, then you'll remember to help them when they need it.

Remember This
Do for other people what you would like to have them do for you.   Luke 6:31

To the Grown-Ups
Practicing the Golden Rule doesn't come easily to young children (or to adults!). Praise your child for her attempts to treat others as she wants to be treated. Remember too that your children are learning from how you treat others—probably more than they learn from what you tell them.

Super Helping Hero

A Story about Helpfulness

Julie Ann put on her red cape. She was playing SUPER HELPING HERO!

Her mother said, "Julie Ann, please help me. Take this chocolate pie to Mrs. Miller."

"OK," said Julie Ann.

Then Julie Ann thought, *What if I get there and Mrs. Miller's house is on fire? I'll save Mrs. Miller! That's what! I'll be SUPER HELPING HERO!*

But everything at Mrs. Miller's was just fine.

"Oh, thank you, Julie Ann," said Mrs. Miller. "Would you take these apples next door to Mr. Perry? It would really help me."

"OK," said Julie Ann.

Then Julie Ann thought, *What if I get there and a big yellow lion is growling at Mr. Perry's door? I'll save Mr. Perry! That's what! I'll be SUPER HELPING HERO!*

But everything at Mr. Perry's was just fine.

"Oh, thank you, Julie Ann," said Mr. Perry. "Would you take this book next door to Mrs. White? It would really help me."

"OK," said Julie Ann.

Then Julie Ann thought, *What if I get there and a raging river is flooding Mrs. White's house? I'll save Mrs. White! That's what! I'll be SUPER HELPING HERO!*

But everything at Mrs. White's was just fine.

"Oh, thank you, Julie Ann," said Mrs. White. "Would you take Tommy home to play with your little brother? It would really help me."

"Sure," said Julie Ann.

Then Julie Ann thought, *What if a ferocious orange tiger is growling at my little brother? I'll save him! That's what! I'll be SUPER HELPING HERO!*

But when she got home, everything was fine. Julie Ann felt sad.

"What's the matter?" asked Mother.

"I wanted to be SUPER HELPING HERO,
but I only
took a pie to Mrs. Miller,
took apples to Mr. Perry,

took a book to Mrs. White, and
brought Tommy to our house."

Then Julie Ann thought. She straightened her
red cape and grinned. "Why, I *am* SUPER
HELPING HERO!"

"That's right," Mother said, "and when you help
others, it's like helping Jesus. It makes Him
very happy—and it makes me happy too. I love
my SUPER HELPING HERO." And she gave
Julie Ann a big hug.

Kids-Life™ Questions

• What would you do if a ferocious orange tiger were growling at you?

• Why do you think Julie Ann wants to be a super helping hero?

• What did Julie Ann do that made Jesus very happy?

From the Bible

Jesus said, "A man was going down from Jerusalem to the

city of Jericho. Robbers came out after him. They took his clothes off and beat him. Then they went away, leaving him almost dead. . . . Then a man from the country of Samaria came by. He went up to the man. As he saw him, he had loving-pity on him. Luke 10:30, 33

Julie Ann was a Super Helping Hero just like the man from Samaria.

Prayer

Dear God,
Today I want to be a SUPER HELPING HERO by

_____.

In Jesus' name. Amen.

I Love Grandpa

A Story about Love

I love Grandpa.

I help him work.
I water the flowers
and pull the weeds
and wash the car.

I love Grandpa.
I let him read my books and play horsey
with me.
I take him on long walks.

I love Grandpa.
I let him buy me ice cream.
I take him to the zoo and share my
friends with him.

I love Grandpa.
I am kind to his friends.
I sit very still in church—
for a few minutes.

I love Grandpa.
I go right to bed and let him tuck me in.

Thank You, God, for Grandpa.

Kids-Life™ Questions

- How do you know the girl in the story loves her grandpa?
- How can you help your grandpa or grandma?
- What do you like to do with your grandpa or grandma?

From the Bible

[Jesus said,]

"Love each other as I have loved you." *John 13:34b*

Prayer

Dear God,

Thank You for giving me grandmas and grandpas to love. In Jesus' name. Amen.

How Many Jawbreakers?

A Story about Honesty

Since the first day of school, a glass jar full of delicious jawbreakers had been sitting on Mrs. Allen's desk. Some lucky person would win that jar, and I really hoped it would be me, Andy Jackson.

• • • • • • • • • • • •

We were supposed to estimate (that's a fancy word for guess) just how many jawbreakers were in the jar. The boy or girl with the closest estimate would get to keep the jar and the jawbreakers. Mrs. Allen said we would write down our answers this afternoon.

After lunch we went outside to play kickball. Mrs. Allen forgot her whistle and asked me to go back and get it.

I ran back to the room and found the whistle on her desk. Right next to the whistle was a small note. I turned it around so I could read it. It said, "732 jawbreakers." I couldn't believe my luck. It was the answer to the contest!

I grabbed the whistle and rushed out of the room. During the kickball game I kept thinking about the note. I know how many jawbreakers there are. I'm going to win! The jawbreakers will be mine!

Then I started thinking about something else. To write 732 on my paper would be cheating. But I really wanted those jawbreakers. "Jesus," I prayed, "help me do what's right."

After the game we all went back to class. Mrs. Allen said, "OK, boys and girls, this is it. You've used your best estimating skills and have come up with a number. Write down your name and answer on a sheet of paper. . . ."

I couldn't decide what to do. The jar would be mine—if I cheated. Everyone else was passing their papers forward. Finally, I wrote down 237, just the opposite of the 732 I saw on the note. I was sad that I wouldn't win, but at least I felt good inside knowing that I did what was right. I know Jesus was happy too.

At last Mrs. Allen said, "I've looked at all your estimates and there were a lot of close ones, but the winner is—oh, wait. Christy had to leave early today, and she left her guess on my desk."

I couldn't believe it! That was the note I saw on the desk.

After looking at Christy's answer, Mrs. Allen said, "There were 232 jawbreakers. The closest estimate was 237 by Andy Jackson. Congratulations, Andy! How did you come up with 237?"

"It was an honest guess, Mrs. Allen. A real honest guess!"

Kids-Life™ Questions

- Why was Jesus happy with Andy?
- How do you feel when you make a good decision like Andy did?
- How do you think Andy felt knowing he won honestly?

From the Bible

A good man is known by his truthfulness; a false man by deceit and lies.
Proverbs 12:17 (TLB)

Prayer

Dear God,
Help me to be honest and tell the truth in all that I do today. In Jesus' name, Amen.

Solomon John and the Terrific Truck

A Story about Unselfishness

Solomon John was the littlest one. His oldest brother drove a car and climbed mountains with a rope.

"Dave the Brave," said Solomon John.

"How's my man?" said Dave.

Solomon John's next oldest brother rode a skateboard and had a secret club that met in a tree.

"Bart the Brat," said Solomon John.

"Babies can't join the club," said Bart.

One day the mailman brought a box from Grandma. There was a leather baseball mitt for Dave. There was a Zippy-Speedo-Whammer-Riffic truck for Bart.

There was a jack-in-the-box for Solomon John. "That's a baby toy," said Bart.

"Can I look at your truck?" asked Solomon John.

"No, it's MINE. Go play with your baby toys," said Bart.

Solomon John's fingers itched. They wanted to touch the Zippy-Speedo-Whammer-Riffic truck.

Bart pushed the truck down the hall to his room. He left it sitting on the floor. Solomon John crept into the room. He touched the Zippy-Speedo-Whammer-Riffic truck with one finger.

"What are you doing in MY room?" yelled Bart.

Solomon John went to his room. He crawled under the bed to his secret place. Jesus was the only One who could find him there. "Jesus," he said, "why don't You teach that Bart to share?"

Then he heard the ice-cream man coming down the street. He had two quarters in his pocket. A Fudgsicle would make him feel better.

The ice-cream man stopped at the curb. "I would like a double Fudgsicle, please," said Solomon John.

"Hey, buddy," said Bart, "can I have some of your Fudgsicle?"

Solomon John felt like saying, "It's MINE." He licked a chocolate drip off his finger.

"PULLEEZZZ?"
said Bart.

Solomon John thought about Jesus. Jesus said to treat others the way you want them to treat you. He wondered if Jesus meant even Bart the Brat.

"Okay," he said. He broke the Fudgsicle in two.

"Hey, you're not such a bad kid," said Bart. "Want to play with my Zippy-Speedo-Whammer-Riffic truck?"

"Sure," said Solomon John.

"I get the first turn," said Bart.

Kids-Life™ Questions

- How do you think Jesus felt when Solomon John and Bart called each other names?
- Do you have a secret place where only Jesus can find you?
- Do you think it was easy for Solomon John to share his Fudgsicle with Bart?
- When is it hard for you to share?

From the Bible

"There is a boy here who has five loaves of barley bread and two small fish." . . . Jesus took the loaves and gave thanks. Then He gave the bread to those who were sitting down. The fish were given out the same way. The people had as much as they wanted.
John 6: 9, 11

Prayer

Dear God,
Sometimes it's hard to share, especially when it's my favorite. Please help me to share today.
In Jesus' name, Amen.

Grumpy

A Story about Thankfulness

Grumpy. That's what Susie called her brother. His real name was Jimmy, but he was grumpy. Even when others were nice to him.

When Susie asked him to play a game, he grumped, "I don't feel like it."

When Tommy wanted to ride bikes with him, Jimmy grumped, "I'd rather watch TV."

When Mom said she would bake chocolate chip cookies, Jimmy grumped, "Why don't you make lemon bars?"

Because he always sounded so grumpy, Jimmy made others feel grumpy too.

"I didn't want to play with you anyway!" cried Susie.

"I'll ride my bike with Pete!" shouted Tommy.

"I won't make cookies if you always complain about them," said Mom.

Susie didn't play with him. Tommy didn't play with him. So Jimmy played alone. And no one baked cookies.

Jimmy tried reading his comic books. But he could hear Tommy and Pete riding their bikes outside. He could hear Susie and Karen laughing and playing a game.

Jimmy went outside and sat down on the steps. He watched Tommy and Pete play ball together. He squeezed his eyes shut so that he wouldn't cry.

Then Jimmy remembered something important. He remembered that God could help him. So he prayed, "God, I'm sorry I've been so grumpy. Please help me not to be a grump. Amen."

Jimmy ran to Tommy and Pete. "Can I play with you? Please?"

Tommy looked at Pete. Then he looked at Jimmy. "Promise not to complain?"

"I promise," said Jimmy. He knew God would help him. Jimmy played with Tommy and Pete for a long time. He didn't feel grumpy at all. Instead he felt very happy.

The three boys sat down on the steps to rest. The door opened and Mom came out. She gave Jimmy a big plate of chocolate chip cookies for everyone. Susie and Karen came out with lemonade for everyone.

"Thank you, everybody," said Jimmy.

Then he whispered, "Thank You, God," so softly that only God could hear.

Kids-Life™ Questions

- Why do you think Jimmy was so grumpy?
- How does it make you feel to be around a grump?
- Why do you think Jimmy felt like crying?
- Name some things you are thankful for that you can remember the next time you're grumpy.

From the Bible

Always give thanks for everything to our God. Ephesians 5:20 (TLB)

Jonah was in the stomach of a fish, but he wasn't grumpy! He thanked God for what he had, just as Jimmy did.

Prayer

Dear God,
Thank You for always loving me, even when I'm grumpy. In Jesus' name, Amen.

Belinda and the Blue Bear Curtains

A Story about Helpfulness

A car rattled down the street and bounced into Belinda's driveway. Out of the car popped Grandma. Out of the house popped Belinda.

Grandma had come to make blue bear curtains for baby Eric's room. And Belinda was going to help.

Daddy carried Grandma's sewing machine up to Eric's room. Grandma carried a big roll of blue cloth covered with blue bears. Mama carried Eric. Belinda couldn't carry those heavy things.

Eric howled, "Yeow-ow-ow!" when Mama put him in his crib.

"I'm sorry," Mama said. "But I must measure the windows."

Belinda reached as high as she could. But she couldn't reach high enough to measure windows.

Daddy set up the ironing board and turned on the iron. Belinda was never allowed to touch the iron.

Grandma snipped away at the roll of cloth, and Mama pinned the pieces together. Belinda tried to help pin. But she pricked her finger. "Oow-eee!"

Grandma ran the sewing machine at top speed. Belinda sat beneath it and let the soft blue bear cloth fall on her. In her room she had lots of cuddly bears. But she didn't have a blue bear.

Daddy put up curtain rods. He told Grandma, "God gave you a talent for sewing."

Mama hugged Grandma. "We're glad you're using your talent to help us."

Grandma said, "God gives special talents to everyone. He wants us to use them to help others."

Belinda sighed. She wasn't sure what her talent for helping was. She guessed it wasn't to help make curtains!

Thump! Eric dropped a sailboat on Belinda. Then Eric reached for sharp scissors. Mama snatched them away.

"Yeow-ow-ow!" Eric's face turned the color of Belinda's bear that looked like strawberry ice cream.

Suddenly Belinda cried, "I know how I can help!" Belinda ran to her room. She hurried back carrying a brown bear, a white bear, a black bear, and a bear that looked like strawberry ice cream.

Belinda held the bears for Eric to see. "Yeow . . . " Eric began to howl.

But Belinda made the cuddly brown bear tickle Eric's tummy and dance along the crib. Eric laughed and laughed.

"Why, Belinda," said Mama. "What a good helper you are."

Belinda laughed too. At last, she found her own special way to help make the blue bear curtains.

Kids-Life™ Questions

• What did Belinda want to do?

• Why do you think Belinda wanted so badly to help?

• What is your special way to help your family?

From the Bible

And Moses, Aaron and Hur went up to the top of the hill. When Moses held up his

hand, Israel would be winning . . . Moses' hands
became tired. So they took a stone and put it under
him, and he sat on it. Then Aaron and Hur held up
his hands, one on each side. His hands did not move
until the sun went down.
Exodus 17:10b-12

Belinda helped her family just as Aaron and Hur
helped Moses.

Prayer

Dear God,
Thank You for all the different ways I can be a
helper. In Jesus' name, Amen.

Kids-Life™

Me and My World

Hey, Kids!

The following stories are about kids like you. Maybe they will make you say, "He's a lot like me!" They talk about what kind of a person God wants you to be.

Think about It

What kind of person are you, on the inside? Are you the kind of kid the teacher can count on to finish his work? Does your friend know you'll do what you said you would do? God will help you become that kind of person. Talk to Him about it, and talk to your favorite grown-up about it too.

Remember This

Happy are the people who live pure lives. They follow the Lord's teachings. Psalm 119:1 (ICB)

To the Grown-Ups

Perseverance, self-image, and responsibility are big words to apply to a young child. But as children take small steps in these areas, they'll mature into godly men and women who have character. Your love and support is vital—so are your prayers for them in this world that often teaches them just the opposite character traits from those you want them to have.

My Mom Loves Me

A Story about Love

On Monday Mark said, "I don't want to go to school."

"I know," his mom said.

"I don't want you to go to work," Mark said.

"But I have to," his mom answered. She took out a tissue and pressed a big, red kiss tight in the middle of it. She slipped it in Mark's pocket. "I love you," she said. "Jesus loves you too."

"I know," Mark said.

Mark showed the tissue to his teacher and said, "See, my mom loves me."

On Tuesday Mark's mom hugged him and said, "I love you."

Mark reached in his front pocket. His mom's big, red kiss wan't there. He reached in his back pocket and pulled out a tissue. Right in the middle was his mom's big, red kiss.

On Wednesday, Mark wondered where he'd find his mom's big, red kiss. He looked in his front pocket. He felt in both his back pockets. The kiss wasn't there. When Mark opened his potato chips, there was a tissue with a big, red kiss. He knew his mom loved him.

On Thursday, when Mark felt in his pockets, there was no big, red kiss. He opened his lunch. No kiss there, either. He wondered where it could be.

After lunch Mark played in the sand. When he was done, he emptied out his shoes. Out tumbled the tissue with his mom's big, red kiss.

On Friday Mark looked through all his pockets, but his mom's big, red kiss wasn't there. He looked in his lunch, but the kiss wasn't there, either.

At rest time, he unfolded his rug. There was his mom's big, red kiss. He knew his mom loved him.

After his rest, Mark painted a picture of his mom with a big, red smile. Then he painted one more thing.

When his mom picked him up, Mark showed her the picture. Then he gave her a paper towel folded tight. When she opened it, there was a big, red kiss. "I love you," Mark said. "Jesus loves you too."

"I know," his mom answered, giving him a big kiss. This time right on his cheek.

Mark was glad Jesus had given him a mom to love him.

Kids-Life™ Questions

- How did Mark know his mom loved him?
- How did Mark show he loved his mom?
- How do you show love for your family?

From the Bible

Love takes everything that comes without giving up.
Love believes all things. Love hopes for all things.
Love keeps on in all things.
I Corinthians 13:7

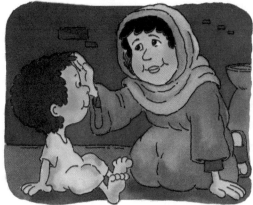

Prayer

Dear God, thank You for giving me people to love
me. Help me to show I love them every day.
In Jesus' name, Amen.

Ellie's Prettiest Jewelry

A Story about Self-Image

Ellie loved jewelry.
She thought it made her look special.

She loved pearl necklaces.
She loved gold bracelets.
She loved sapphire earrings.
She loved ruby rings.
She loved emerald pins.
She even loved silver anklets.
And she especially loved diamond tiaras.

Ellie began to wear more
and more
and more
and more jewelry.
She never went anywhere without it.
But then she discovered something.

Jewelry gets in the way.

It's hard to play baseball with too much jewelry.

It's hard to chase your brother with too much jewelry.

It's hard to jump rope with too much jewelry.

It's almost impossible to swim with too much jewelry.

And too much jewelry is very distracting in church on Sunday.

Finally Ellie decided to do something about it.

She took off her diamond tiara.
She took off her silver anklets.
She took off her emerald pins.

• • • • • • • • • • • •

She took off her ruby rings.
She took off her sapphire earrings.
She took off her gold bracelets.
She took off her pearl necklaces.

Mother said, "Now you're wearing the jewelry
God gave you."

"Where?" cried Ellie. "Where is it?"

Mother said, "I can see pearls in your smile,
sapphires in your eyes,
golden sunbeams sprinkled in your hair,
and God's love over you like a diamond tiara."

Kids-Life™ Questions

- What did Ellie discover about her jewelry?
- What did she decide to do?
- Ask someone in your family what is special about you.

From the Bible

Then [Ruth] got down with her face to the ground and said to [Boaz], "Why have I found favor in your eyes? Why do you care about me? I am a stranger from another land."

Boaz said to her, "I have heard about all you have done for your mother-in-law after the death of your husband. I have heard how you left your father and mother and the land of your birth to come to a people you did not know before. May the Lord pay you for your work. Ruth 2:10-12a

Ruth did not wear fancy clothes or jewelry. She was loved for who she was and what she did.

Prayer

Dear God,
Thank You for making me so special on the inside.
In Jesus' name, Amen.

My Special Job

A Story about Responsibility

One sunshiny day, Nathan decided to play in his sandbox. He got out his shovel, his trucks, and his pail.

"Remember to clean up when you're done," Mother told him.

Nathan nodded. He knew God gave each person special jobs to do. Picking up his toys was Nathan's special job. Mother said it was his *responsibility*.

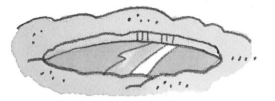

First Nathan dug a hole with his shovel. He used his pail to fill the hole with water. That made his hole look like a lake. Nathan jumped into his lake. He wiggled his toes in the sand. It felt cool and squishy.

"Nathan," Mother called. "It's time for lunch. Please clean up and come inside."

After playing all morning, Nathan was hungry. Quickly, he put his shovel in his pail. He parked his trucks near his sandbox.

Looking around, Nathan smiled. All his toys were picked up. He had done his job well. God would be pleased, and so would Mother.

"I'm ready for lunch," Nathan called proudly.

But Mother shook her head. "Before you can go inside and eat, there's one more thing to clean up."

Nathan pointed to his toys. "But everything is put away."

"Your toys are neat," Mother said with a smile. "But something still needs cleaning up." Bending down, Mother brushed the sand off Nathan's shorts. "Before we go inside, we have to clean up you!"

Kids-Life™ Questions

• What was Nathan's special job?

• What are some of your special jobs?

• Why was God pleased with Nathan?

• How can you do your jobs so God will be pleased with you?

From the Bible

So Saul said to his servants, "Find me a man who can play

well, and bring him to me." One of the young men said, "I have seen a son of Jesse the Bethlehemite who plays music well. He is a man with strength of heart, a man of war, wise in his speaking, and good looking. And the Lord is with him." I Samuel 16:17,18

David had a special job too. His special job was to play music for Saul.

Prayer

Dear God,
Thank you for my special jobs. Please help me do them the best that I can. In Jesus' name, Amen.

Don't Give Up!

A Story about Perseverance

Kurt waved good-bye to Mother. As he ran toward his classroom, he looked down. His shoelace was untied.

Kurt asked Mother to tie it. Mother frowned. "Can you tie it yourself?"

Kurt shook his head. "Tying shoes is too hard."

"Giving up won't make it easier," Mother told him. "You have to keep trying." But when Kurt sighed, she bent down and tied his shoe.

"Thanks!" Kurt called and ran into his classroom.

The children were crowded around a glass box. Kurt saw an egg inside the box.

A yellow beak poked through the eggshell. "A baby chick!" Kurt cried. But the beak disappeared.

Kurt's teacher clapped her hands. "While the chick is resting, let's have our arts and crafts time."

Kurt painted a picture of the egg. When he was finished, he leaned on the table and watched the chick. Its beak poked through the hole. Then a long crack crept around the egg. The beak disappeared again!

"It's playtime," called his teacher.

As Kurt ran toward the sandbox, he thought about the chick. Why had it quit pecking?

When playtime was over, Kurt emptied the sand from his shoes. "Teacher," he called. "Please tie my shoes."

"I thought you could tie them yourself," she said, bending down.

"It takes too long," Kurt complained. "I want to see the chick."

Kurt hurried inside to watch the egg. Wet feathers were poking through the hole now.

But after story time, the hole wasn't any bigger. Kurt frowned. Would the chick ever get out of its shell? "Please, God," he prayed. "Help the chick keep pecking."

When rest time was over, Kurt rushed to the glass box. Bits of shell lay around the egg.

"Look!" Kurt cried. The egg was moving. Suddenly it cracked in half.

"The chick made it!" shouted Kurt. Everyone cheered.

At snack time Kurt prayed, "Thank You, God, that the chick kept pecking."

As Kurt bit into his cookie, he noticed his shoe. It was untied. He started to call his teacher. Then he remembered the chick. It didn't give up. The chick had worked and worked until the shell broke open.

Bending down, Kurt tried to tie his shoe. He tried again. Finally he smiled. The bow wasn't as neat as Mother's, but his shoelace was tied.

Kurt looked at the chick. "Sometimes you just have to keep trying," he whispered. As the chick stirred and looked around, Kurt was sure he saw it nod.

Kids-Life™ Questions

- Why do you think the chick quit pecking?
- Why do you think the chick made it out of its shell?
- What is something that is hard for you to do?

From the Bible

Let everyone be sure that he is doing his very best, for then he will have the personal satisfaction of work well done, and won't need to compare himself with someone else.
Galatians 6:4a (TLB)

Prayer

Dear God,

It's really hard for me to _____. Please help me to keep trying, just like Kurt and the chick.

In Jesus' name, Amen.

When I Get Bigger

A Story about Self-Image

Jesus made me small. But He is helping me grow bigger.

There are a few things I can't do yet, like get my favorite teddy bear mug from the top kitchen shelf.

Or write a letter to Grandpa George and mail it all by myself. But someday I will!

Today I can't bake chocolate chip brownies alone, or pour cranberry juice from my mom's pretty new glass pitcher. But someday I will!

I can do things today that I couldn't do when I was smaller. And there will always be new things to learn.

So, if today I can't—that's okay. Because someday I will!

Someday I will button and bake and cut and paint all by myself. Someday I will be older and taller. Someday I will read God's Word, the Bible, all by myself.

Someday I will grow stronger and faster because that's the way Jesus planned it. He planned that I would grow and learn and think and do.

Why, I'm even growing this very minute! And if you can't tell by looking at me today . . . someday you will!

Kids-Life™ Questions

• What are some things you can do now that you couldn't do when you were smaller?

• What do you wish you could do now—all by yourself?

• What will you be able to do when you get bigger?

From the Bible

You saw me before I was born and scheduled each day of my life before I began to breathe. Every day was recorded in your Book!
Psalm 139:16 (TLB)

Prayer

Dear God,
Thank You for all the things I'm big enough to do now, like _____. In Jesus' name, Amen.

Johnny's Lost Shoes

A Story about Responsibility

"Hurry," said Daddy, "and we'll all go to the fair."

"Oh, boy!" shouted Johnny as he ran up the stairs.

Johnny put on clean jeans and a clean shirt. He put on his left sock. He put on his right sock. But he didn't put on his shoes. He couldn't find them.

"Mama!" cried Johnny. "My shoes are lost. I looked and looked, but they aren't anywhere."

"Dear God, please help Johnny find his shoes," Mama prayed. Then she said, "Why don't you look under your bed?"

Johnny looked under his bed. He found his football. He found his favorite book. But he didn't find his shoes.

"Why don't you look in your sandbox?" asked Mama. Johnny ran outside and looked in his sandbox. He found two of Mama's spoons. He found his favorite dump truck. But he didn't find his shoes.

"Why don't you look in the car?" asked Daddy. Johnny ran outside to the car. He found a wrapper from a hamburger. He found a map that no one could fold up the right way. But he didn't find his shoes.

"Why don't you look in Ginger's doghouse?" asked Mama. Johnny ran outside and looked in Ginger's doghouse. He found the smelly blanket she slept on. And a flea found Johnny! But he didn't find his shoes.

"Did you look in your closet?" asked Daddy. Johnny looked in his closet. He found a crumbly old cookie. He found one of Ginger's chewed-up bones. Guess what else he found!

"Thank You, God, for helping me find my shoes," said Johnny. "They were right where they belong. Now I can go to the fair!"

Kids-Life™ Questions

• If you looked in your closet right now, what do you think you would find?

• Have you ever lost something? What was it?

• Who can help you when you lose something?

From the Bible

And [God] knows the number of hairs on your head! Never fear, you are far more valuable to him than a whole flock of sparrows.
Luke 12:7 (TLB)

Prayer

Dear God,
Thank You for caring about everything, even a lost pair of shoes. In Jesus' name, Amen.

Jake's Birthday Surprise

A Story about Patience

Everyone was always telling Jake to be patient.
When Mom baked cookies she said, "Jake, be
patient or you'll burn your mouth!"

But chocolate chip cookies were Jake's favorites.
So he'd eat one quickly.

And, sure enough, the cookie burned Jake's
tongue. "OW! WOW!" he yelled.

When Jake and Dad played ball, Dad called,
"Wait for the ball, Jake!" But Jake couldn't wait.
And he swung the bat too soon.

Even Jake's grandmother told him to be patient.
"Jake, your birthday will be here soon enough."

Jake wanted a parakeet for his birthday. He
hoped Grandmother would buy one for him.
"How many days?" he asked.

At last Jake's birthday was here! And, sure enough, Grandmother arrived with a parakeet in a cage.

"Just what I wanted!" Jake cheered.

The parakeet went, "Peep, peep."

"I'll name her Peeper," Jake said. "I'll teach Peeper to talk and to ring a bell! But first I'll teach her to sit on my finger."

"It will take time," Dad said.

Mom said, "You will have to be patient, Jake."

"I will," Jake promised.

Jake carried Peeper into his room. Then he opened the cage door. "Good bird," he said gently. He put his hand near the opening.

"Peep! Peep!" Peeper tweeted loudly.

"Don't be afraid," Jake said. He moved his hand inside the cage.

Jake placed his finger near Peeper's perch. "Get on, Peeper!"

Peeper flapped her wings wildly. But she did not get on Jake's finger. Jake wanted her to hop on right away. So he forced his hand against Peeper's chest. And . . .

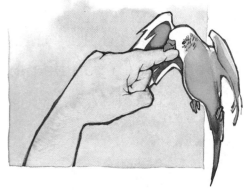

Peeper bit Jake's finger! HARD! "OW! WOW!" Jake wailed.

Mom came running. "Peeper bit me!" Jake cried.

Mom shook her head. "Jake . . ."

"I know," Jake said. "I wasn't patient."

That night Jake's dad said, "Why don't you ask God to help you be patient?"

So Jake prayed, "God, help me to be patient. Especially with Peeper."

In her cage Peeper tweeted, "Peep, peep."

The next morning Jake put his hand inside Peeper's cage again. "Don't bite me, Peeper," he said softly. Peeper cocked her head. But she did not bite Jake or hop on his finger.

Jake was patient—even though Peeper didn't get on his finger for two days. Then it happened. On Friday, Peeper flapped her wings and hopped right on!

"Good bird!" Jake laughed. "Next I'll get you a bell. But not today. You have to be patient!"

"Peep," Peeper agreed.

Kids-Life™ Questions

- How was Jake patient?
- What happened because Jake was patient?
- What are some ways you can be patient?

From the Bible

But when the Holy Spirit controls our lives he will produce this kind of fruit in us: love, joy, peace, patience, kindness, goodness, faithfulness, gentleness and self control.
Galatians 5:22, 23a (TLB)

Prayer

Dear God,
Please show me how to be patient when I want something to happen soon. In Jesus' name, Amen.

Kids-Life™

Special Days

Hey, Kids!

The following stories are all about holidays. They'll help you remember why you celebrate these special days.

Think about It

What is your favorite holiday? Who do you celebrate it with? Special days are good times to praise God for the good things He gives us. But you don't have to wait for holidays to praise God. Right now, praise God for three things that make today a special day! You can praise Him with a Bible verse, a song, a prayer, a picture, or in a way just your own.

Remember This

Sing to the Lord a new song. Sing to the Lord, all the earth. Sing to the Lord and praise his name. Every day tell how he saves us.   Psalm 96:1, 2 (ICB)

To the Grown-Ups

Make praise a way of life in your home. Even on a dreary, mundane day, stop and praise the Lord. It will lift everyone's spirits and remind your family of all the good things God gives to you.

I Know Why We Have Easter

A Story about Easter

My name is Judith. I live in Jerusalem. Let me tell you about Jesus. He is my friend.

I first saw Jesus when He was teaching some people out in a grassy field. I was there with my mother. My friends and I wanted to go and talk to Jesus.

But one of His helpers tried to send us away. "No," the helper said. "Jesus doesn't have time for children. He's a busy man."

Jesus heard him tell us that. "No, no," said Jesus. "Don't send the children away. Let them come to Me."

Some of the littlest ones climbed onto His lap. I stood right in front of Him.

Jesus put His hand on my head and smiled at me. He said, "The kingdom of God will be made up of people who are like these little children."

Jesus became my friend forever.

It seemed that everybody loved Jesus then. But after a while, lots of people didn't like Him anymore.

They said bad things about Him. The bad things were not true, but people believed them. And they began to say, "Crucify Him."

And that is what happened. They put Him on a cross and killed Him.

I cried and cried.

But that's not the end of the story. It's only the beginning. Because . . .

• • • • • • • • • • • • • • • •

JESUS DIDN'T STAY DEAD!

He was buried in a cave, in a garden. On Sunday morning, just as the sun was rising, some women went to visit Jesus' grave. When they got there, the grave was open, and Jesus was NOT THERE!

An angel was sitting on the stone that had closed the grave. The angel said, "Jesus is not here. He is risen."

Mary Magdalene was one of the women who visited the grave. She is my mother's friend. She was so excited when she told us about it.

"I was standing there crying," she said, "when a man came up to me. I thought he was the gardener. I said, 'Sir, tell me where you have taken the body of Jesus.' "

"Then the man said, 'Mary.' And I knew! I knew it was Jesus Himself! I couldn't believe it. But it was true. I saw Him with my own eyes. He is alive!"

I knew that my friend Jesus was not dead. I was happy.

Jesus visited with His helpers after that. Then one day, He went up, up, up, and disappeared into the clouds.

Jesus had told His helpers that He would go to live in heaven with God, and He did.

I'm glad that Jesus is still alive. He is alive forever. That's why we have Easter Sunday.

Happy Easter!

Kids-Life™ Questions

• If you could see Jesus right now, what would you ask Him?

• How do you think Jesus felt when people were saying bad things about Him that weren't true?

• Why is it so special that Jesus rose from the dead?

From the Bible

The angel said to the women, "Do not be afraid. I know you are looking for Jesus Who was nailed to the cross. He is not here! He has risen from the dead as He said He would." Matthew 28:5, 6a

Prayer

Dear God,

Now that I know why we have Easter, please help me to tell others about it. In Jesus' name, Amen.

Moms Are Special

A Story for Mother's Day

Moms are special people.

Moms never get tired.

Moms can make anything
out of cardboard boxes.

Moms appreciate nature . . .
most of the time.

Moms don't always let you win.

Moms have quick reflexes.

Moms know what you're up to.

Moms are there when you need them.

Moms are understanding. (Usually.)

Moms believe in you.

Moms can be a little bit embarrassing.

Moms cry at the oddest times.

Moms never run out of hugs.

Moms are one of God's best ideas!

Kids-Life™ Questions

- What do you like doing with your mom?
- How do you show you love your mom?
- Show her you love her today!

From the Bible

*. . . Obey your father and
your mother. Tie their
instructions around
your finger so you won't
forget. Take to heart all
of their advice.*
Proverbs 6:20, 21 (TLB)

Prayer

Dear God,
Thank You for my special mom. In Jesus' name, Amen.

All About Daddies

A Poem for Father's Day

Dear God, the Bible says You're our daddy.
Are You just like my daddy, God?

When I fell down and scraped my knee,
My daddy picked me up.
Will You be there to pick me up, God?

The other day I helped my grandpa put pictures
 in his album.
That made my daddy really happy.
Are You happy when we help each other, God?

I had a bad dream last night.
My daddy came in and made the scaries go away.
Can You make scaries go away, God?

Last fall when we moved from our old house I was very sad.

My daddy held me tight and made me feel happy again.

Do You make us feel happy again, too, God?

In the spring, my daddy and I planted flowers in
    our new backyard.
We took care of them and helped them grow.
Do You know how to make flowers grow, God?

I wanted a kite to fly on windy days, but I didn't
    tell anyone.
My daddy got me a kite—it was a big surprise.
Do You like to surprise us too, God?

One time I got really, really sick.
My daddy had to carry me around the house.
Do You ever carry Your children, God?

I asked my daddy all these questions about You,
    God.
He said that You do
Pick us up, and
Like it when we help, and
Chase the scaries away, and
Help us feel happy, and
Make flowers grow, and
Surprise us, and
Even carry us.
Wow, You're a really great daddy, God!

Kids-Life™ Questions

- When does your dad make you feel happy?
- How does your dad show he loves you?
- God loves you even more than your dad loves you. Draw a picture or sing a song to God to tell Him you love Him too.

From the Bible

See what great love the Father has for us that He would call us His children.   I John 3:1

Prayer

Dear God,
Thank You for my special dad and for being the most special dad of all. In Jesus' name, Amen.

The Very Special Baby

A Story about Christmas

Right this very minute, this very day, and every minute of every day all over the world new babies are being born.

Some are girl babies.

Some are boy babies.

Some babies are born in the morning, some in the afternoon, and some at night when the stars are twinkling and the moon is glowing.

Some babies sleep in big cribs, in big nurseries, in big houses.

Some babies sleep in small beds, in little rooms, in tiny houses.

No matter where they sleep or when they are born, all babies are special.

You are special.

One night a very long time ago in a town far from here called Bethlehem, a baby boy was born.

The baby was more special than all other babies. This baby was God's own Son.

"What should I name this very special baby?"
His mother had wondered.

God sent an angel who spoke in a voice as
beautiful as a song.

"You shall call Him Jesus," said the angel. Jesus means "God will save us."

So the baby's mother obeyed the angel. She named God's Son Jesus.

Then she kissed Him and hugged Him and gently laid Him in His little bed made of straw.

A big bright star was shining in the sky right above the place where baby Jesus slept.

Ever since that long ago and faraway night, people all over the world celebrate the birthday of baby Jesus.

We call that day Christmas. And mothers and fathers turn on bright lights to remind us of the star that shone over the place where Jesus was born.

"Happy birthday, Jesus," we sing to God's Son.

Now every baby boy and every baby girl born every minute of every day can know that God sent His very own Son to be with us.

He was a very special baby.

The Savior—yes, the Messiah, the Lord—has been born tonight in Bethlehem!

Kids-Life™ Questions

- What does the name Jesus mean?
- Why did Mary name her son Jesus?
- When do we celebrate Jesus' birth?

From the Bible

"The Savior—yes, the Messiah, the Lord—has been born tonight in Bethlehem!" Luke 2:11 (TLB)

Prayer

Dear God,
Thank You for sending us the most special baby ever.
In Jesus' name, Amen.

Christmas Is Jesus

A Story about Christmas

Christmas is God
Who gave us His Son
And sent Him to earth
So His plan would be done.

Christmas is angels
Announcing the story
Telling the shepherds
"To God be the glory!"

Christmas is shepherds
Who came when they heard
Then shared joy with others
And spread the glad word.

Christmas is wise men
Who came from afar
And traveled until
They came to the star.

Christmas is Mary
Who was Jesus' mother.
She knew at His birth
He was like no other.

Christmas is Joseph—
Jesus' father on earth
Who shared in the joy
Of this little boy's birth.

Christmas is Jesus
Come down from above
Sent by the Father
To show us His love.

Kids-Life™ Questions

• What does Christmas mean to you?
• What does your family do at Christmas?
• What did God give us at Christmas?

From the Bible

For to us a Child will be born. To us a Son will be given.   Isaiah 9:6a

Prayer

Dear God,

Please help me show Your love to others this Christmas. In Jesus' name, Amen.

ACKNOWLEDGMENTS

ALL ABOUT DADDIES: written by Christina Rose Murschel, illustrated by Bari Weissman

BELINDA AND THE BLUE BEAR CURTAINS: written by Mary Reid, illustrated by Kathy Mitter

CHRISTMAS IS JESUS: written by Joanne Schlange, illustrated by Jean Arnold

DON'T GIVE UP!: text © 1990 Marlys G. Stapelbroek, illustrated by Bron Smith

ELLIE'S PRETTIEST JEWELRY: written by Jacquelyn Calvert and Janet Noonan, illustrated by Karen Godkin

GOD GIVES US COLORS: written by Carolyn Owens, illustrated by Jane Conteh-Morgan

GOD MADE EVERYTHING—JUST RIGHT!: written by Karen Bigler, illustrated by Bartholomew

GOD WHISPERS TO ME: written by Louise H. Kohr, illustrated by Terry Julien

THE GOOD SHEPHERD: written by Kersten Hamilton, illustrated by Benton Mahan

GRUMPY: written by Berit Kjos, illustrated by Bartholomew

HOW MANY JAWBREAKERS?: written by Terry Thornton, illustrated by Bartholomew

I KNOW WHY WE HAVE EASTER: written by Evelyn S. Wilharm, illustrated by Benton Mahan

I LOVE GRANDPA: written by Don Fay, illustrated by Bari Weissman

JAKE'S BIRTHDAY SURPRISE: written by Charlotte Graeber, illustrated by Terry Julien

JESUS—MY VERY BEST FRIEND: written by Kersten Hamilton, illustrated by Jill Trousdale

JOHNNY'S LOST SHOES: written by Marylin Young, illustrated by Rosemary West

KIDS-LIFE™ illustrations by Rick Incrocci

MOMS ARE SPECIAL: written by L. B. Norton, illustrations © 1988 Bartholomew

MY FAVORITE KIND OF LOVE: written by Lou Ann Smith, illustrated by Anne Kennedy

MY MOM LOVES ME: written by Carol Green, illustrated by Susan Nethery

MY SPECIAL JOB: text © 1990 Marlys G. Stapelbroek, illustrated by Anne Kennedy

SOLOMON JOHN AND THE TERRIFIC TRUCK: written by Kersten Hamilton, illustrated by Raoul Soto

SUPER HELPING HERO: written by Barbra Minar, illustrated by Paul Harvey

THE VERY SPECIAL BABY: written by Lou Ann Smith, illustrated by Benrei Huang

WHEN I GET BIGGER: written by Lou Ann Smith, illustrated by Toni Hormann

Some stories and illustrations were previously published as Little Butterfly Books, Little Butterfly Shape Books, and Sparklers.

*T*hese commandments that I give you today are to be upon
your hearts. Impress them on your children. Talk about them
when you sit at home and when you walk along the road,
when you lie down and when you get up.
Deuteronomy 6:6, 7 (NIV)

Parents—

Are you looking for fun ways to bring the Bible to life in the lives of your children?

Chariot Family Publishing has hundreds of age-appropriate, fun-to-read-and-use books and toys that teach Christian virtues including obedience, faith, love, thankfulness. They will help you teach your children the Bible and apply it to their everyday lives. Here is a sampling of the educational, inspirational, and fun products you will find at your local Christian bookstore.

The Kids-Life™ Bible

Lots of easy-to-understand stories to read alone or with Mom or Dad to help children learn the truths of God's Word.

The Big Big Big Boat (and other Bible stories about obedience)
Yea, Hooray! The Son Came Home Today (and other Bible stories about wisdom)

Timeless Bible stories (three in each book) that are fun to read. These stories help children learn biblical values while being entertained.

/

Let's Talk about Heaven
Bible-based answers to children's most-asked questions about our forever home.

The True Princess
A wonderful parable about a princess who learns what it means to be a loving servant as Jesus taught.

Kid's Bible Challenge
Here's a fun trivia game that teaches children about the Bible.

Pocket Kids Choices Game
Fun with a plus! One hundred game cards designed to reveal a child's spiritual development.

Noah's Memory Match-Up Game
Players learn the Bible story of Noah as they match pairs of cards displaying Noah, his family, and the animals.

Chariot Books
A Division of Cook Communications

Rainfall

Look for these and other exciting products
from ChariotVICTOR . . .

Parents, are you looking for fun ways to bring the Bible to life in the lives of your children? ChariotVICTOR Publishing has hundreds of age-appropriate, fun-to-read-and-use books and toys that teach Christian virtues including obedience, faith, love, thankfulness. They will help you teach your children the Bible and apply it to their everyday lives. Here is a sampling of the educational, inspirational, and fun products you will find at your local Christian bookstore:

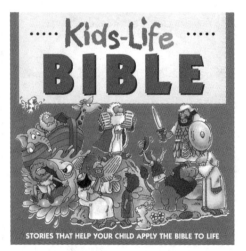

Kids-Life Bible
by Mary Hollingsworth.
A new dimension in children's Bible reading. With lots of easy-to-understand stories to read alone or with a parent, this book helps children learn the truths of God's Word.

ISBN: 0-78143-020-8
Retail: $12.99